Enjoy Fishing!

enjoy living!

by Maury DeYoung

Scriptures taken from the Holy Bible, New International
Version®, NIV®. Copyright © 1973, 1978, 1984, 2011
by Biblica, Inc.™ Used by permission of Zondervan. All
rights reserved worldwide.
www.zondervan.com.

Library of Congress Control Number: 2011961998

ISBN: 978-0-9725539-1-9

First Printing, January 2012

Additional copies of this book are available by mail.

Maury DeYoung
PO Box 88336
Grand Rapids, MI 49518
mdeyoung@spi-int.org
www.spi-int.org

Printed in the U.S.A. by
Grandville Printing Company
4719 Ivanrest Ave. S.W.
P.O. Box 247
Grandville, MI 49468
1-800-748-0248

TABLE OF CONTENTS

DEDICATION

TO GOD

Who gives us this amazing world to enjoy, especially for the gift of his son Jesus Christ, who enables us to enjoy living.

TO MY WIFE, CHERYL

As time goes on, I am more and more amazed at the woman you have become. I thank God for you. I appreciate the precious memories that we share, which even includes some special times of fishing together. You are a wonderful mother and grandmother to our children and grandchildren. Your Godly example allows them to see what it means to enjoy living.

TO OUR CHILDREN

Chris & Arlene, Gene & Michelle, Tom & Lisa, Tim & Nikki

Life for me is very satisfying as I see how you have matured and how you choose to live for God. This book would not exist except for the times we have shared together in the out of doors and the encouragement and assistance you have given to me in putting this together.

IN MEMORY

Derrick Joel DeYoung – our youngest child

Although you left this world so quickly in a car accident when you were only 16 years old, you taught me in your short life, what it means to enjoy living. Now I cannot even imagine how enjoyable life is for you in heaven. We miss you...

TO OUR GRANDCHILDREN

Joel, Natalie, Alex, Lucas, Mikayla, Zachariah, Tiffany, Noah & Fisher

God gives me great enjoyment in spending time together with you especially in the outdoors. I trust that you will each learn how God can help you enjoy living life to the fullest.

TO MY MOTHER

From an early age, you and Dad taught me to trust in God and live for him. Now you still encourage me. I thank you for your many prayers.

IN MEMORY

Clayton E. Knoll - Bud

When your pickup first arrived at our driveway at 5:30 am on that first Wednesday morning, neither you nor I realized what a deep friendship would develop between us and how God would help us to mentor each other as life went on. I am grateful.

FORWARD

These fishing stories are based on actual outdoor experiences, as I remember them. Many of these stories came from times spent with members of my family. Others came from outdoor experiences with friends. Some of these came from activities out of Sportspersons Ministries International.

With each story, I have tied in devotional thoughts based on principles from the Bible. I hope they will enable you to take a fresh look at Christianity and see how God can enable you to enjoy living.

In this book you see a variety of pictures. Many of these pictures illustrate the point of the story and tie in with the devotional. You also find many pictures of children. I am convinced that spending time with children is extremely valuable, which includes your own children, your grandchildren, children of friends or a child you are mentoring. Through these experiences you can build lifelong memories.

I also believe values are more caught than taught. In an outdoor setting you have the opportunity to demonstrate good values that will be passed on to those you care about. Take a child fishing with you at an early age, and you will be amazed at the value of doing this.

Although many people have encouraged me and assisted with this project in many ways, I will highlight a few that need extra recognition.

First of all, I want to thank my niece, Deb Rozeveld for doing such an outstanding job in the layout of this book. I appreciate your willingness to help and your creative touch to make it easier to read.

I thank my family. Each of you has contributed in so many ways - participating in the stories, encouraging me, giving me ideas and suggestions, and then especially for Arlene, Lisa, and Shelly for the editing and proofing that you did.

Thanks to the others who helped with editing and proofing and gave other suggestions and encouragement: my sister-in-law, Carol Christians, some dear friends, Mark and Mari Romanack and Keith and Lynn Kavajecz, and a former teacher, John Rozeveld.

Photographs. Most of the photographs were taken by the author. I appreciate the ones that were submitted by my family members. Thanks to Deb Rozeveld and Mark Romanack for the pictures you allowed me to use. We appreciate the permission granted for the pictures on the back cover from Kevin VanDam, Mark Romanack, Keith Kavajecz and Lance Valentine.

INTRODUCTION

Enjoy living. I understand that we live in a broken world with lots of hurt and disappointment. We live under a lot of stress and the future is uncertain.

As I talk about enjoying life, I am not trying to escape from this reality. Instead, in the midst of these challenges, I am trying to lay a foundation for how life can be much more enjoyable as we connect to God and respond to him properly.

As you read these stories, I hope you also can see that Christians can have pure fun and find pleasure in living. It's my desire that this book will assist you in discovering a deeper satisfaction in living.

ENJOYMENT

How many times have we been in the outdoors when we thought, "it can't get much better than this." We are awestruck by the beauty.

We relax in the peaceful, quiet atmosphere. The adrenaline rushes with the thrill and the excitement of the catch. Think about a couple of times when you have experienced something like this in the outdoors.

Some people seem to think that all pleasurable experiences are wrong. "Pleasures" must be sinful.

The Bible gives us a much healthier perspective. It shows that some pleasures can be sinful. It talks about the fleeting pleasures of sin. They can be enjoyable but they don't last. And afterward there is brokenness, shame, and guilt.

On the other hand, there are good, clean, fun filled, enjoyable experiences that are gifts from God!

"...to put their hope in God, who richly provides us with everything for our enjoyment."

We can enjoy living because God gives us so much to enjoy in life.

We can enjoy experiences, because these are gifts from God.

It's like God gives us a taste of enjoyment now on this earth, but he also reminds us that heaven will be enjoyable.

"...with eternal pleasures at your right hand."

Don't participate in fleeting pleasures of sin, but live life to the fullest and give thanks to God for everything he allows us to enjoy. I hope you are looking forward to an enjoyable, pleasurable experience in heaven. ⓧ

REFLECTION

1 TIMOTHY 6:17 PSALM 16:11
HEBREWS 11:25

COURAGE

It amazes me how courageous outdoors men are to try certain things. A few years ago we were in Canada fishing for a week with our kids. About the middle of the week, they had to take us to a spot to show us something. We thought they were showing us another good fishing spot. Instead, they had tried out something the day before. While we thought they were just out fishing, they decided to do some cliff diving. They did put some safety factors in use. They probably knew that if they would have asked us dads first, we would put a stop to it. After all, isn't it easier to ask forgiveness than to ask for permission? I'm not recommending this for everything!

As men tell their fishing and hunting stories, there is a lot of courage expressed (although sometimes it appears to be more stupidity than courage). Risk...the higher the risk, the more attractive it becomes! What could be more thrilling than fishing in a location where you might have to look back to see if a bear is approaching? Or look at how many river fishermen move closer and closer over the slippery rocks to the "deep hole" risking a cold bath instead of catching the big one.

The Bible talks about courage in a variety of ways. Moses, the great leader of God's people, told Joshua, the new leader who was taking his place,

"Be Strong and Courageous."

Moses informed him that God would go before him, would be with him, and would never leave nor forsake him. God himself reaffirmed this same message to Joshua as he

began to lead God's people. As Joshua learned this lesson by experience, he continued to pass this same message on to the people he was leading (and now to us as well),

> *"Be strong and courageous. Do not be afraid; do not be discouraged, for the Lord your God will be with you wherever you go."*

God knew the challenges would be huge and the battle would be demanding, but God expected courageous men to go forth and claim the territory.

Jesus chose some courageous men to be his closest followers. He too, knew that the challenge would be great and the battle intense. The risk would be dangerous, but God would go before them and be with them. He needed courageous men to advance his kingdom!

There is another passage in the Bible that talks about

the opposite of courage...people who are cowardly. In fact it is a pretty strong statement showing how "cowardly" is unacceptable to God. In a list of those who will not be included in heaven, it lists such lifestyles as those who are "unbelieving, vile, murderers, sexually immoral, those who practice magic arts, idolaters, and liars." But I skipped one category. Do you know what is mentioned first on this list? "The cowardly..." If one of those categories fits you, it doesn't mean that you cannot be forgiven and that you will not be able to repent and turn to God. However, if you have not trusted in Jesus Christ as your forgiver and asked him to be your leader, but instead continue in your unbelieving ways and go on with a lifestyle like is mentioned above, don't expect to be accepted in heaven.

If we analyze what it means to be cowardly, we would have to say that it is the same as not believing or not trusting in God to take care of us or help us. No wonder God doesn't like it for people to be cowardly.

How would you place yourself on the scale between cowardly and courageous? Perhaps we need to take another look at what God wants and what he promises, and then step forward in the challenging, risky, dangerous cause of advancing his rule on this earth. ⚪

REFLECTION

REFLECTION

JOSHUA 1:7-9   REVELATION 21:8

HEAVY FOG

Early morning often seems one of the best times for fishing, especially as summer wears on. Fishing usually isn't very good in the middle of the day, often morning or evening is best. You have probably gotten up early to go fishing, and when you arrived at the lake you noticed there was a fog settled over the lake.

Sometimes fog can make things look very beautiful. What a gorgeous sight to see a light mist rising over the water as the sun comes up. Other times the fog can be so thick that it's hard to see where we are going. We can see only a short distance ahead of us. If we are driving to the lake, the low areas are especially difficult. But even on the lake, we need to exercise extreme caution in heavy fog.

I think life is often like that, religiously, for some people. God doesn't seem very clear or real to them. I recall one man who lived for years as if God lived in a heavy fog. This religious stuff didn't make sense and he didn't want any part of it. Sure, he believed in a supreme being. He believed there was some power behind the universe. After all a wonderful world like we live in, couldn't have just happened accidentally.

But beyond that, God was in a fog to him.

Then one day the fog lifted, and he discovered that God was very real. He saw what God had to offer: forgiveness, peace, purpose, new meaning, deeper friendships, and a fantastic future besides.

As the fog lifted, he felt so embarrassed, guilty, and

ashamed – when he compared his life to what God expected. He knew that he certainly didn't have an acceptable mixture to offer up to God. Yet he realized that God loved him and offered him forgiveness for all the mistakes he had made. He realized that Jesus Christ made the difference. Jesus had paid the penalty for all his mistakes, by suffering, shedding his blood and dying on the cross.

Perhaps you have been living in a fog. God seems so unclear. There must be a higher being of some sort, but you certainly don't know much about him. I urge you to strain through the fog, just like when you are driving a car or boat in the fog. Search God out, try to find him. Seek and see if God is real and what he might have to offer you.

God will honor your search. Listen to what he says,

"You will seek me and find me when you seek me with all your heart."

If you are still in the fog religiously, I urge you to seek God with all your heart. Remember, a half-hearted search may not produce the results you are looking for. God says that you can find him,

"...when you seek me with all your heart." ✕⟩

REFLECTION

JEREMIAH 29:13

PASSION

I am intrigued by the passion of outdoor people for the sports they enjoy. I'm not talking about the passion related to testosterone, but how much they seek after and pursue their area of interest.

Outdoor interests vary from those pursuing a record book buck or other big game, to those who chase steelhead or their bigger "relatives" in the deeper water. We could list a variety of other pursuits.

Passion for outdoor interests is demonstrated in many ways. People watch videos or read about the sport they enjoy. They attend seminars at sport shows, they buy certain clothing, they talk to other experts in the field, and they spend lots of time on the water or in the field. Many outdoor people keep journals or take pictures and later analyze them to become more effective at the sport they enjoy.

However, when it comes to another area of life, many people seem to have a weak connection to God. Most outdoors people believe in some type of higher power. If one spends time in the outdoors, it's hard not to believe in some type of designer behind this amazing world we enjoy. But most outdoors people don't have a very close or passionate relationship with God.

Sometimes God seems far away because of our lifestyle. We put him at a distance. We know our behavior doesn't match what he would want, so to relieve our conscience we push God further and further away.

The God who designed and created this amazing world, is also the same God who loves, is gracious, is forgiving and is merciful. It is possible to connect with him in a deeper way.

Listen to what the Bible says:

"Seek the Lord while He may be found, call on Him while He is near."

That sounds a lot like passion to me. When you become passionate in your pursuit of God, you will find him! If God seems distant, maybe it is time to become more passionate in your pursuit of God. Seek him with all your heart! ✕◯

■ REFLECTION

REFLECTION   ISAIAH 55:6

ANCHOR

It was starting to get dark. We were casually riding around the lake before going inside. As we came near the public access, we noticed something that looked rather strange. As we got closer, we saw what it was. A boat was upside down in the water!

We quickly headed over to see if anyone needed assistance. On the shore stood a young man, dripping wet.

We stopped to see if he was alright, if anyone else was involved, and if he needed any help. He indicated that he was alone and was unharmed. Just cold and soggy.

As we talked with him he explained what had happened. He had borrowed his grandfather's boat for the evening to fish for some panfish.

He found a spot right near the public landing where the fish were biting. He put down the anchor and decided he would fish there for a while. Everything seemed to be going well, until he went to pull up the anchor and leave. That's when he got into problems. He was a large young man in a small, flat bottom boat. The anchor that his grandpa had in the boat, was simply a cement block attached to a rope.

I don't know if his grandpa had used that anchor before. But this time, when his grandson lowered the anchor, it ended up buried in the soft muck at the bottom of the lake.

The anchor was attached to the front corner of the boat.

This young man went to that corner and took ahold of the rope and he began to pull. In fact, he pulled very hard. He was strong, but the anchor wouldn't budge. So he tried even harder to pull it out. Instead of freeing the anchor, he literally pulled the boat over. His weight shifted and overboard he went as the boat capsized! He was able to swim to shore and was trying to decide what to do next, when we found him.

He was concerned because he not only was using his grandpa's boat; he was using his grandpa's fishing equipment. He was afraid that when the boat tipped over, all his grandpa's tackle and equipment went down to the bottom of the lake.

How would he explain this to his grandpa?

We joined in to help him. After finding how stuck the anchor was, we decided to cut the rope and leave it there. It was deep enough. It would not bother any boats coming in, and besides that, it was totally submerged in the mud! We then floated the boat to shore where we could get a better grip to tip the boat back to its right side. As we tipped it over, we found out that the life jackets had caught all the fishing gear as the boat tipped. All the tackle was still under the boat! Nothing was lost (except the anchor)!

I imagine most of us have not used a cement block for an anchor in an area of a lake where the bottom is soft. But, I suspect we all are guilty of some foolish fishing mistake. It seemed like the right thing to do at the time, but later you realized how senseless it was.

When it comes to daily living, we have all made some unwise choices in life. In fact, we have all made some immoral decisions. These decisions have hurt us. Some have caused hurt to others. We have all disappointed God and fallen short of his expectations. Some of these may be private activities which no one else knows about. Others mistakes may be very public – like when the man was caught standing on shore soaking wet.

The Bible says:

> **"...for all have sinned and
> fallen short of the glory of God."**

Just like we had to assist this young man out of his disaster, so too, we need someone to help us get out of our messes. We need to be rescued!

Jesus Christ is the only one suitable to come to our aid.

The Bible says:

> **"If we confess...**

admit, own up to

> **...our sins, he is faithful and just and will
> forgive us our sins and purify us from all
> unrighteousness."**

Will we trust him to forgive us and then clean us up on the inside? ✕◯

REFLECTION
REFLECTION

ROMANS 3:23   1 JOHN 1:9-10

BOAT LAUNCH

What a mess! They had been fishing and had a good time together, but now it was time to leave. They drove the boat back to the launching area. Dad went and got the truck and trailer and backed it down the ramp. He then got into the boat so he could load it on the trailer. He asked his son to get into the truck to drive it ahead when it was loaded.

Everything was going well. He drove the boat up onto the trailer and called to his son to put it in drive and move forward. He told him to "give it some gas" so the truck would pull the boat up out of the water.

That's when the trouble came. Somehow, the son slipped the brand new, full-size, dually truck into reverse, instead of drive. He stepped on the gas and proceeded to back the truck right into the water. Of course, this launch dropped off quickly and it didn't take long before the truck was almost submersed with water - right up to window level! The boy even had to climb out of the window!

As they stepped back and looked at their situation, they decided to call a friend, who also had a large truck, to come over and help pull them out. It didn't take very long and their trucks were hooked together with a very heavy chain. As he was trying to pull the truck and boat trailer out of the water, the tow chain broke. A piece of chain flew forward, wrecking his friends' tailgate, and continued right through his back window, just missing his head. Talk about a bad day!

Eventually they called a tow truck. The tow truck came and attempted to pull out the rig. It was interesting to watch. With each tug, they had to stop and let the water drain out before they could try to pull it any further. Repeating this every six to twelve inches made it quite a process, but they finally got it out!

I'm not sure how the father and son handled that mistake. This truck was brand new. He had purchased it about two weeks before and now it was ruined! Water had even gotten inside the cab. Most of the motor and electronics were covered with water. They can be thankful no one was hurt.

Mistakes! We have all made them. Some of us still live with the consequences of poor choices. Not only foolish, but wrong choices. We have not even satisfied our own moral or ethical code. And we would have a rather weak résumé if it were to be reviewed by God.

Wrong choices = sin. The Bible says:

"All have sinned and fall short of God's glory."

It says:

"There is none righteous, no not one. We have all turned aside, we have all gone astray."

The amazing message of the Bible is that God doesn't leave us alone to solve our messes. He provided the solution for sin, so that he can forgive us. This doesn't mean that he waves some magic wand to remove all our consequences, but he does offer to clean us up on the inside, giving us the opportunity to have a new start.

Are you still struggling with a poor choice you made? Will you turn to God and ask him to forgive you? Then ask him to start changing you from the inside out. ✗◯

REFLECTION

ROMANS 3:10-11   ROMANS 3:23

MINNOW BUCKET

We were on a weeklong fishing trip in Canada with a group of relatives. At first we had difficulty finding fish, but our fishing improved each day.

One afternoon one of the men went out to fish for some walleyes in one of the bays that he could enter about one fourth of a mile from our camp. Before he went, he asked my brother-in-law if he could use his minnow bucket, and he took it along with some minnows to jig for walleyes. While he was fishing in the bay, he hung the inside of a metal minnow bucket over the edge of the boat with some minnows in it. Somehow it got loose and disappeared while he was fishing.

After fishing for a while he came into camp and told my brother-in-law that he owed him a minnow bucket. He explained what happened and offered to buy him a new one when we got back home.

We continued to fish for the rest of the week. We had a great time together and caught a lot of fish.

Friday morning was pack up time. We had to check out shortly before noon, so we began to clean out our cabins. We also had fished the night before, so we had to clean out our boats and make sure we didn't leave any important items in them. I was walking with a couple of our kids down to clean the boats, when we noticed something in the water. As I looked more closely, I could hardly believe what I saw. There, rocking back and forth in the shallow water near shore, was my brother-in-law's minnow bucket. It was obviously his because he puts his initials on all his equipment. We walked over, picked it up, and opened the cover. Not only had the minnow bucket drifted back to our shore right next to our boats, but the minnows were still alive and were still swimming in it! I don't know how that bucket got back to the shore at our camp from the bay where it was lost earlier in the week. Somehow it returned and was found!

As I reflect on this experience it reminds me of our lives. We get "lost" in some distant bay. We make reckless mistakes, we make bad choices, we mess up, sin, and find ourselves "lost." We drift far away from God. We experience brokenness, often because of our mistakes, and live with guilt and shame. We have to endure the consequences of our actions. Sometimes we drift around in a far off bay for a long time.

But the good news of the Bible is that God is able and desires to lead us back to camp!

This is what the Bible says about our sins:

> *"But your iniquities have separated you from your God; your sins have hidden his face from you."*

But God's love is overpowering and in grace he reaches out to rescue us:

> *"Remember at that time you were... without hope and without God in the world. But now in Christ Jesus, you who were once far away have been brought near through the blood of Christ."*

Where are you now? Are you enjoying a close relationship with God and benefiting from friendship with God's people? Or are you still lost out in some distant bay? Perhaps you are starting to head back to camp, but it is taking a long time to get reconnected to God and his family.

Let God lead you home! Trust in Jesus Christ and follow his leading and you will be surprised how much better your life will be. ✗○

REFLECTION

ISAIAH 59:2   EPHESIANS 2:8, 9, 12-13

FISHING GLOVES

Many fishermen use fishing gloves at one time or another. Perhaps you are fishing in cold weather and you use gloves to keep your hands warm.

You might have a glove that assists you in handling the fish; either to protect the fish or to protect your hand. Some of you might use a glove when filleting fish.

Fishing gloves can smell pretty bad. We may not notice it when we have been fishing for hours and catching quite a few. But let someone who hasn't been fishing come near those gloves. You will probably have to get them out of there!

In many ways our lives are like dirty fishing gloves. We may not notice it right away, but if we take a step back, we aren't so "clean." We have made mistakes, have to suffer the messy consequences, or live with the guilt of what we have done. God offers to wash us clean. A song puts it this way:

"What can wash away my sin?
Nothing but the blood of Jesus."

Blood represents the life of a creature. Jesus Christ shed his blood and suffered and died for a purpose. A perfect sacrifice had to be made to satisfy the justice of God so that we could be forgiven. Jesus Christ was the only one who qualified. We can become clean and fresh and new again, as if we never sinned. In order for that to happen, we need to trust in God's method, trusting what Jesus has done for us, instead of trying to find our own cleanser which will never get the deepest stains out. Think again of that dirty, stinky, fishing glove. It would be nice if it could be all cleaned up and smell nice again. God can do this in our lives. He can clean us up and forgive us.

But he also wants us to live better now. That's why he gives us his Spirit to live right inside us, when we ask. Just like a hand can enable a glove to do something, so too, Jesus can change our lives, by his Spirit, starting on the inside of our lives, and then affecting others around us as we change for the better.

Will you invite Jesus to wash you clean...to take the stink out of your life? Will you invite his Spirit to remodel you on the inside, and then flow through you to make a positive difference in relationships you have? ✗○

REFLECTION

1 JOHN 1:9   1 PETER 1:18-19
1 CORINTHIANS 6:19-20   JOHN 1:12

WHICH WAY

It was a pleasant afternoon. A young man from the church asked if we could go fishing some evening for walleye. We worked things out and this was the night. We used a 14 foot fishing boat with a small outboard. This was big enough for the lake where we would be fishing. He said he knew the lake well enough to get us into good fishing areas.

We met and headed to the lake. He thought it would be best to start by the boat launch near the marsh. After we got the boat into the water, and parked our vehicle and trailer, we headed out to fish. Actually, the launch area was really in the marsh. The marsh grass was at least 8 -10 feet high in most of the area. We had to maneuver through this channel of marsh grass to get out to the lake to the area where he wanted to fish.

This posed no problem and we headed out to fish. We fished for a couple of hours, but just were not catching anything. This young man knew people had fished this area the night before and had caught several. We figured the bite might pick up as it began to get dark.

The evening was so peaceful. Why not stay just a little longer? Walleyes can sometimes bite better at night, especially in a shallow lake. Unfortunately, the only bites we got that evening were mosquito bites. We eventually gave up and headed in. By this time it was very dark.

We headed back toward the boat launch and suddenly faced a new challenge. Remember, we came through a channel in the marsh to get to the lake. Now, as we headed back, there seemed to be all kinds of channels in the marsh grass! Everyone we took ended up a dead-end. Over and over we tried to get out, but kept running into a barrier of marsh grass. We had one small flashlight but the batteries were getting low and it didn't give us enough light to find the right exit. We tried for over an hour without success. Too bad the boat launch was not lighted!

Eventually the young man with me thought of a plan. He knew where the swimming area was, and that it was not too far from where our car was parked. He was quite sure that if we went back out to the lake, he could find the swimming area. I could then drop him off close to shore and he would go and get the car. He could then shine the lights down the boat launch, so I could see where the channel was and head to the right place.

That is exactly what we did. We headed back out to the lake again. There was just enough moonlight to see the swimming area, so his plan was unfolding. I dropped him off in shallow enough water that he could walk to shore instead of swimming. I waited a few minutes until he got to the car and started it, and then watched as he shone the lights down the launch area. Then I headed back to the marsh area. It still took a couple of tries before I found the right channel, but eventually I got there. We loaded the boat and headed home (about two hours after we had planned).

When it comes to religion, people think there are many roads to connect to God. They think that as long as people are sincere in their belief, they will all end up in the same place. Jesus, on the other hand, claimed to be the only way to God.

"I am the way and the truth and the life. No one comes to the Father except through me."

Christianity is based on the fact that Jesus lived, died, and rose again. After that He ascended into heaven. He is the only one qualified to pay the penalty for our sin, so that we can be right with God. He can give us a better life now and a wonderful future with him in heaven!

If you examine most other religions, they are really lacking in comparison to Christianity in what they offer for the present life and for the future. Besides that, all other religions are based on a leader who died. Christianity claims that Jesus Christ not only died, but arose from the dead. After that he ascended into heaven.

Don't keep heading down dead end channels spiritually. Turn to Jesus, the one who is "the light of the world." Let his light lead you to the right connection with God. ✗⟶

REFLECTION

JOHN 14:6   JOHN 8:12

GONE

We were fishing on a pontoon. My partner decided to fish in the back of the boat, so I went to the front. I took two fishing poles with me. The first was a new rod and reel combo that I had just purchased. The other was an older one that I had been using for some time. I set them up with different lures so I could switch off.

I laid the new combo in the corner of the boat, making sure it was out of the way so that no one would step on it. I went to the other side of the boat and started fishing. After a few casts, I reeled my lure in. Then I made another cast. Only this time, as I cast out my lure, I felt something else get caught. I looked, and somehow my lure had caught my brand new rod and reel combo. I watched helplessly, as it lifted it up into the air, dropped off, and splashed down into the water, reel end first.

I knew there was no hope of recovery. The rod and reel went into water that was 45 feet deep. At that time our electronics were not good enough to find it down there. That new combo was gone! It was buried in the depths of that lake.

The Bible uses a similar image when it describes what God does with our sins when he forgives us.

It tells us he...

"...will again have compassion on us; you will tread our sins under foot and hurl all our iniquities into the depths of the sea."

Imagine all the mistakes, failures, wrong decisions, improper words, actions and even bad thoughts you have had; all of them gone, buried in a land fill or cast into the depths of the sea! Then imagine God putting up a "NO TRESSPASSING" sign, not allowing anyone else to dig them up again. Also see him locking them in an unbreakable container, so all that garbage doesn't pollute the fish in the sea! It's buried in the depths of the sea. Thank God our sins are gone!

Forgiveness is an amazingly wonderful gift! Have you/will you accept God's gift? If you have tell God and show God how thankful you are!

REFLECTION

REFLECTION

MICAH 7:18-19

CLOUDS

Every fisherman has seen clouds. Sometimes the bite is much better with some cloud cover and a little ripple on the lake from the wind.

Cloud cover; it doesn't stay forever. Eventually the clouds move out and the sky clears again. Or you may be out in your boat relaxing and you look up at the sky and see a cloud. If you watch that cloud, you notice that it is moving, and before long, it moves out of sight.

Sometimes life is filled with many good things...some good relationships, some good activities, and lots of other things that are pleasant. You might catch a fish, or land a big one, or even win a tournament. But on the other hand, life for most of us has some clouds hanging around. We also experience, fear, guilt, shame, remorse, and live with consequences of bad decisions.

God has some very good news for us in the Bible.

Think of your sins - the mistakes you have made... that broke your own moral code...that messed up your relationships with others...that put a separation between you and God.

Listen to what He says:

"I have swept away your offenses like a cloud, your sins like the morning mist."

Imagine all the garbage of your life as if it were packed

away in the mist or in one or more of those clouds.

God says...

"I have swept away your offenses..."

They are gone, removed, forgiven, pardoned. What an amazing statement!

But there are a couple of other aspects to what God is saying, that we should not neglect. He also says:

"Return to me..."

Turn back to me. It takes action, a decision on our part to connect or reconnect with God.

And then there is one other thought here.

"I have redeemed you..."

I have paid for you...I bought you back...I paid a price for you.

A lot of people trust themselves. They feel they have done many good things. Perhaps they think they are average or a little above average. There are lots of people who do worse things than them.

Thinking that way is like making an omelet or scrambled eggs for a guest. As you are preparing to fry them, you crack the eggs. You put in the first one. You crack the second, it is rotten and you throw it in. The third and forth are good, so you put them in. The fifth is rotten, and you put that in, too.

You would never do that if you were fixing eggs for a friend, but that is what we think we can offer a holy, pure, sinless God!

We present him with a mixture of good and bad. However, God's standard is still perfection. We can never live up to his standards.

But God provided a solution for us...he paid the price. Jesus Christ paid the penalty for our sin.

Will you trust him?

Will you accept that?

Ask him to forgive you and invite him to help you clean up your act and live a better life.

REFLECTION
REFLECTION

ISAIAH 44:22

CATCH & RELEASE

Many of you practice "catch and release." For trout, bass, and musky fisherman (along with many others) "catch and release" is often the norm.

Recently we had the privilege to fish on Lake St. Clair for muskies. The weather was not very pleasant as storms were moving through the area and the wind had picked up. Our captain offered to let us fish another day, but it was hard to rearrange our schedules, so we decided to try it anyway. In order to find quiet enough water to fish in, our captain decided to take us all the way across the lake. What a day we had for catching muskies! We landed 21 out of 30 hits! Each of us caught a fish that was over 40 inches with the biggest at 49 ½! What incredible fish! What a day! We made sure that we took enough pictures so that people could see what we caught because we were practicing "catch and release." We had the camera ready as soon as the musky was landed so that we could release it back into the water as quickly as possible.

Have you ever thought about this in terms of religion? Have you ever wondered if God practices catch and release? Perhaps you have connected with God at one time, but now you have drifted away. Even after learning more about what God expects, you really messed up! Why would God ever keep you or me?

There are times when we wonder how God could let us back into a relationship with Him after all the times we have failed and disappointed Him. Even when we know better, we have blown it repeatedly! We have not only disappointed ourselves, but know we have also broken

God's standards. The Bible shows that God does NOT practice "catch and release."

Listen to what God says in the Bible:

"I give them eternal life, and they shall never perish; no one can snatch them out of my hand."

Realize what the Bible is saying. When God gives us a free gift – eternal life (which starts now and has a wonderful future), it is like he places us right in the center of His hand. And He says NO ONE – not even you, can take yourself out of that position!

We often think that if we have done something so bad it would cause God to get upset and He would throw us back.

Listen to what the Bible says in another passage (God is telling us this):

"...whoever comes to me, I will never drive away."

God promises that He will never release us!

Now, this doesn't give us an excuse to live any way we want. If we have put our trust for now and eternity in Jesus Christ, we will want to show our thanks to Him for what He has done. He has given us His Spirit, coming right into our lives enabling us to live differently. Changing us first on the inside and then in what we do and say. If we have messed up and made a mistake (or several of them) it's time to tell God we are sorry and then ask for His help to live differently.

"Catch and Release!" Good for fishing, but thankfully God doesn't practice it on us! ✗〇

REFLECTION
REFLECTION

JOHN 10:27-29 JOHN 6:37

RULES

As a family we made a trip back to Iowa where we had lived before. While there we decided to try one of our favorite fishing holes on a river just below a dam.

We took a couple of boys out fishing with us. After we fished a while I noticed the one boy was having some trouble with his reel. Eventually I decided to trade poles with him; I gave him my rod and reel and decided to use his. He had a small closed faced reel that had seen its better days.

We were standing on the shore casting over some wild, rushing current into a pool near the middle. After working with his reel, I finally got it to cast out to the pool. About the time my lure got there, I had a hit! I had a fish on and it wasn't a small one. When it ran, the drag could hardly keep up.

When we fished by that dam previously, we usually caught walleyes or smallmouth bass, but would occasionally catch a northern pike. I figured I must have a northern on.

The kids had moved downstream a bit, so I couldn't let them fight this fish.

The fish made a run and then came back, but he was still on the other side of the rapids. How could I get this big pike across the wild current? I didn't know what test line was on that reel, but from the way it looked, I guessed it was probably about six pound test. Suddenly this fish swam right at me, right through the wild water to my side! I wound that reel like crazy trying to keep up. But he didn't stay there, he made a run downstream again. After a few

more runs, the fish seemed to be tiring, so I put some gentle pressure on him. I tried to work him through the rapids again, and eventually I got him across. Now I could tell he wasn't fighting so much. I continued to work him on my side of the rushing water. Finally he rolled up to the surface. What a nice pike! Of course we didn't take a net along, so I had to continue to work him until he was tired enough that I could pull him up on shore.

We had a tape measure along, so I checked his length. He was thirty-seven inches long! Quite a fish to catch on a small combination. Looking at his body I noticed how big it was! We didn't have a scale with us, but his girth was huge! I took a closer look at this fish. This didn't seem like a northern pike, maybe it was a muskie. The rule book I had with me indicated that I should count the number of holes on the front edges of its mouth. Sure enough, it was a muskie. By this time the kids had gathered around and they wanted to see it. In fact they wanted me to keep it so we could weigh it and get a picture of it (of course, we didn't have a camera near us). The rule book also said that muskies had to be forty inches long to keep, so without any further delay, I gently released him back into the water. The memory is etched into our minds, as that big fish swam back into the river.

I wonder if someone else ever caught that muskie or how big it eventually got.

Rules and regulations. We get a booklet every year. Every year it lists the changes and the new rules or regulations for that year. If we fish in a different state or country, we need to make sure we know the rules of that area before we fish.

When it comes to fish or wildlife in general, rules protect the wildlife. They make it possible that other people can continue to enjoy this sport. Some rules are designed for our safety.

The Bible contains rules and regulations too. It shows us how to live as a Christian.

> *"Love the Lord your God with all your*
> *heart and with all your soul and with all*
> *your strength and with all your mind; and,*
> *'Love your neighbor as yourself.'"*

It is not that God is trying to make us miserable. Instead, he wants to protect us from getting hurt and he wants us to enjoy a full satisfying life. Some rules are designed to improve relationships. Life will work best when you do it God's way.
✖◯

REFLECTION

DEUTERONOMY 6:4-6 LUKE 10:27

ELECTRONICS

Today, electronics can play a major role in fishing. You may start your trip using a GPS unit in your vehicle to get to the lake. Then, once you get on a lake, electronics are almost necessary unless you are very familiar with that particular lake.

Fishermen use everything from flashers that help identify depth changes, to very complex units that are preloaded with topographical lake maps and GPS. Some people even use camera equipment to see what is below them.

Electronics have changed a lot of methods in ice fishing as well. Instead of drilling lots of holes and moving often, good electronics allow you to determine the best place for fishing.

Professional fishermen rely heavily on electronics to identify promising areas when pre-fishing. These electronics track their route and allow them to come back to the same place during a tournament. Two of my friends take a vacation each year to fish walleyes. A few years ago, they located an area in the lake where they caught several nice walleyes. Each year they use their GPS and return

to the same spot and continue to have similar success.

When it comes to fishing, we rely so quickly and heavily upon electronics as our guide, but when it comes to living we so often ignore the most helpful guide for life. The Bible is a relevant guide for daily living and also tells us how we can have a wonderful future.

> **"All scripture is God-breathed and is useful for teaching, rebuking, correcting and training in righteousness."**

The Bible is God's message to us. It shows us what the right road is, how we get off track, how we can get back on the road, and how we can stay on the right road; religiously, that is.

There are many ways we can learn from the Bible. One way is to read a Psalm each day and if you have time, also read a Proverb. Let the day of the month determine which Psalm and Proverb you read.

In the Psalms you see how the author was very genuine in his relationship with God. Perhaps it will help you to be more real in your relationship with God.

Proverbs is wisdom literature, which offers good advice for living. You will be surprised by how much the Bible can make a difference in your life! ☓〇

REFLECTION

II TIMOTHY 3:15-17

SUCCESS

S uccess. What would make your fishing trip successful?

This past summer we spent a week up in Canada with my brothers-in-law and some of our children. We had a great time and shared lots of good stories. We had decent weather and were catching fish. But one thing bothered us. We had chosen this lake because it was supposed to have a good amount of large pike. Now we had been fishing a few days and were catching lots of walleyes, but only caught a couple of small pike. Some of our group had worked extremely hard trying almost every method we could think of to catch pike and we had no success. Finally we decided that a number of our group would portage to a nearby lake and see if we could catch some pike there. This proved to be successful, but we did not hook into any large ones. The next day another group went back there and again caught several pike, but nothing very large.

The week provided many wonderful memories and we were able to eat a lot of fish and take some home besides. Probably the best memory for the kids was cliff diving. They had found a steep cliff with deep water below it and decided to try cliff diving. They first tried the lower level at about 14 feet and then moved up to the higher spot at about 45 feet. They tried to make it as safe as possible, but as parents we still had some concerns as we watched our kids jump or dive into the water. For the kids, this experience certainly climaxed the memories of this trip, but I believe there was still a lingering disappointment that we caught so few pike and were not able to get into any large ones.

Success. What do you consider a successful fishing trip - whether that is one evening, a full day, or perhaps a full week? For some, just getting out may make it successful, just the chance to get away. Perhaps you are fishing with a family member or a friend and that makes it successful. Perhaps catching a fish makes it successful for you. For some of you,

though, I suspect success means catching a certain size fish or a certain species.

The Bible talks about success and describes it in a different way than what we usually think. When Joshua became the new leader of the Israelites after Moses died, he received these instructions which I believe still are valid for us today. God promises:

"Do not let the Book of the Law...

That is referring to the Bible.

"...depart from your mouth; meditate on it day and night, so that you may be careful to do everything written in it. Then you will be prosperous and successful."

The Bible indicates that success comes from being very familiar with what the Bible says, focusing on it, and applying it to our lives. That's a little different definition than catching the right kind of fish or getting an expected raise or promotion at work.

But if we think about it, the Bible is filled with lots of practical, life-related ideas that are designed to make life work better. We can be at peace with God, enjoy improved relationships, and live with a clear conscience. That sounds like successful living to me.

Perhaps we have been focusing in the wrong place for success. Let's make sure we spend enough time investigating, reading, meditating, and applying what the Bible says; and then we will discover what successful living is like. ✖

REFLECTION

JOSHUA 1:8

SHARP HOOKS

I remember with embarrassment an experience from a few years ago. I was fishing with some of my kids in a fishing tournament sponsored by our club. After some time my daughter had a bass hit the new chartreuse spinner bait I had put on her line. She cast into some lily pads and suddenly a monster bass came rocketing out of the water after her lure! He jumped so high, we could all see him. What a sight. Picture perfect! This was a bass bigger than I had ever caught. But when it came out of

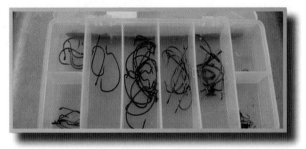

the water, the bass shook his head and the spinner bait went one way, and the bass the other. He disappeared underneath a lily pad. I told my daughter to quickly cast out there again, just beyond that spot to see if he would hit it once more. Sure enough, he hit another time! Up he came, not quite as high as the first time, but with the same result. The spinner bait went flying the opposite direction. Would this same bass hit it yet again? I didn't expect it, but she tried. This time he wasn't as aggressive, he just left a big swirl as he touched the bait again, a little tug and then he was gone.

After the third time, I asked my daughter if I could check her lure to see if her hook was bent or something. She had

a brand new spinner bait on, so the hook should be sharp. I looked at her lure and then I immediately noticed what was wrong. The hook was not bent; instead it was still covered with a clear plastic hook guard that I had not removed! There was no way she could have hooked any bass!

I still look back at that time with regret and embarrassment. What a difference a sharp hook would have made. It would have been such a thrill for my daughter to land that bass. And it easily would have won the tournament.

What about your hooks? I'm sure you are not as careless as I was to leave a hook guard on a lure. But do you fish with sharp hooks? Do you sharpen them before you use them, or do you make sure you buy the sharpest hooks for fishing?

Do you realize that something else is very sharp? The Bible, God's word to us can penetrate deep into our lives, convicting us of something we have done wrong. This may be uncomfortable, but it is best to get something toxic out of our lives. The Bible can also encourage us when we are down, comfort us when we face a loss, and give us direction when we are confused. Read it and see how sharp it is. Listen to God speaking to you personally through his word.

"For the word of God is living and active.
Sharper than any double-edged sword, it
penetrates even to dividing soul and spirit,
joints and marrow; it judges the thoughts and
attitudes of the heart." ✕◯

REFLECTION

HEBREWS 4:12

WHICH LURE

I was fishing in an evening bass tournament that our Sportsperson's Club had sponsored. We usually have three or four tournaments each summer. This particular evening I was teamed up with someone who had fished a lot of tournaments. He said he has fished in approximately three tournaments each week since he was 16 years old and now he has a 16-year-old child.

The biggest challenge of the evening was lure selection. My friend impressed me with his first cast as he landed a decent keeper. The conditions were not good for catching fish. A cold front had moved in and the fish seemed to have lockjaw. My friend had three poles set up and ready. He started with the one that had a crank bait attached. He used a lure that would suspend, and his first cast produced a fish. But he kept trying to catch another one with no success. I tried plastic but could produce only a small bass that wasn't even in the legal size range. I switched to some of the scent impregnated plastics but that didn't help. Later I downsized and that didn't seem to make much difference. My friend also tried a wide selection of lures with no success. Which lure should we try next? The structure was great. He had pre-fished this area with great success, but now things had changed.

Choices – which lure should I use is often a question that we consider when we go fishing. We probably have a couple of lures that we have real confidence in, use these a lot, and go back to them when the going gets tough. We also try different lures when we face new situations, or

when our old dependable ones are not producing.

We face many choices in life. We make many little decisions each day; at other times we make major, life changing decisions. Sometimes we struggle not knowing what is best. Each choice seems to have some good and bad aspects, and we don't know if it's best to stay with what we have or move out into a new challenge.

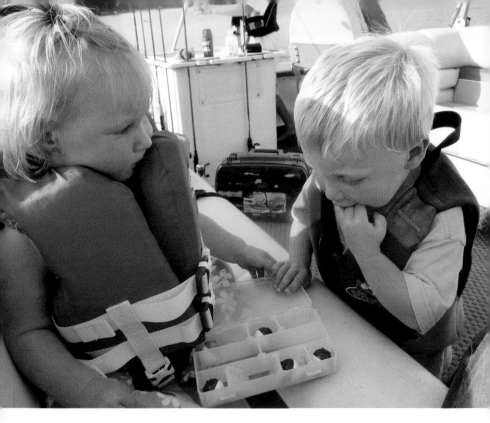

The Bible has a beautiful promise for us when we face decisions. It says that God is willing to give us wisdom. Wisdom means having a good practical sense to make decisions that work best in our lives.

Listen to God's offer:

> **"If any of you lacks wisdom, he should ask of God, who gives generously to all without finding fault, and it will be given him."**

The Bible goes on to say that we should ask firmly believing, and not be like a wavering boat that is tossed back and forth by the waves.

You may have sorted out your options, you may have even asked a friend for advice, but have you gone to God and asked him for wisdom? He promises to give it to you. Did you notice what else that verse said:

"...without finding fault."

God won't make fun of us for not consulting him first or punish us for turning to him as the last resort. We can count on him to help us.

If you are facing some choices in life, turn to the one who can help you, who promises to help you when you ask and believe that he will make a difference. ✖○

REFLECTION

JAMES 1:5-8

SOFT BITE

Fishermen know there is a great difference between catching different kinds of fish. For example, take steelhead, they explode and head down stream almost before you can grab your pole. Consider a smallmouth bass, the moment one is on, he comes flying up out of the water! But with walleyes it is different – especially when jigging. You need a very sensitive rod and a close watch to even notice they are hitting.

A soft gentle touch. Just watch the tip of your rod for a slight change. That reminds me of a story in the Bible.

God was trying to get someone's attention; He was trying to connect with this person. The person's name was, Elijah. But Elijah was trying to run away from God because he was discouraged and depressed.

In the Old Testament God spoke more directly to people, especially to the prophets. Elijah was one of those prophets. Now we have the advantage of having his Spirit teach us; instead of having direct revelations from God.

God came to Eliljah and told him to go stand by the mountain. Suddenly some powerful things began to take place. First, there was a wind that was so strong it began to blow rocks around, so that some even broke apart. That must have been quite a wind!

"...but the Lord was not in the wind."

Then there was an earthquake. Some of you have experienced an earthquake and others of us can at least imagine what it would be like if the ground began to tremble.

"...but the Lord was not in the earthquake."

Then something started on fire and there was fire all around.

"...but the Lord was not in the fire."

I'm sure these things got Elijah's attention. But the next step is even more surprising:

"And after the fire came a gentle whisper."

At that point Elijah suddenly realized he was in God's presence and God was speaking to him.

God didn't speak through the drama of the powerful wind, the earthquake, or the fire, but instead chose to speak through a still small whisper. That's how God often speaks to us today. We read the Bible and as we read or think about a phrase, we can hear his encouragement, instructions, or challenge. His Spirit speaks to us with a very gentle, caring, tender, loving, gracious, merciful whisper, in the ordinary moments of life.

God can use dramatic means to get our attention. But more often, he speaks to us in gentle whispers as we read the Bible or as we discern in our hearts that he has spoken. Are you listening? ✕◯

REFLECTION

1 KINGS 19:9-18

GET THE NET

Get the net! It's easy for us to ask for help when a "big one" is on our line and we don't want to lose it. Perhaps professional bass fishermen get a "bass thumb" from lip handling their fish, but even they get help from their partners. I've seen steelhead fishermen move out of the way to help a fellow fisherman, even giving up their own opportunity to fish to help someone else. I've seen a person position his boat to help his partner land a fish.

Get the net implies, "I need your help!"

Sometimes it is easy to ask for help. Like when you have hooked a big fish. Other times it is very difficult or perhaps even embarrassing to ask for help. We certainly don't want to appear to be weak or inadequate.

However, if we are honest, all of us could use some help. Perhaps something is strained or broken in our lives, or we are not winning over a destructive habit. Perhaps a relationship is stretched to the limit and we know we are in trouble. We may be in a situation where we know we are beyond our self-designed solution.

If you find yourself in a place where you could use some help, don't get discouraged. Help is available, and we should get over our embarrassment of asking for help.

First of all, God offers help. In fact, he provides it day by day.

Listen to what the Bible says:

"Praise be to the Lord, to God our Savior, who daily bears our burdens."

Isn't it amazing! God, who is high and lifted up, the one who is so powerful he is called the Almighty, the indescribable one; still loves us enough to bear our burdens every day!

Will you ask God to get the net? Will you look to him for the help that you need?

God doesn't just wave a magic wand and fix everything to our liking and our demands, but he is there to give us the help we need in whatever situation we find ourselves. What an amazing, caring God we have!

In fishing, when we ask someone to "get the net" we are asking another person for help.

In life, we are so independent, proud, self-reliant; and don't want to appear weak. Perhaps it's because we are so insecure and want to look like we have everything under control, so we don't ask others for help.

In fishing we don't mind asking for help from another person and that doesn't make us look weak. We expect our friends to help. We expect them to come through. We count on them. We not only expect them to grab the net, but they also better handle it well. We don't beg them to position the boat for our advantage. Getting assistance in life is a part of living well, not a sign of weakness.

The Bible says:

**"Carry each other's burdens, and this is the
way you will fulfill the law of Christ."**

Don't try to live life all on your own. Depend upon God daily and turn to a friend you can trust to get encouragement or advice. Will you ask someone to "get the net" to help you in life? ✦

BUGS

We were fishing up in Canada. We had taken a train in and had gotten dropped off at a certain mile marker. As we got out we saw the owners waiting in their boats at the bottom of the hill ready to take us to their resort.

We had a wonderful week of fishing and gained great memories of our time together. We caught a lot of walleyes, several perch, and a few northern pike.

The weather was very comfortable and the bugs didn't bother us very much, during the daytime.

One day I had to make a phone call. There was a telephone pole with a phone on it, near the railroad tracks where we had arrived at the lake. I left the camp and went across the lake to the area where we had first been picked up from the train. Everything seemed alright until I got near the phone. I have never seen so many mosquitoes at one time! Even the head net that I was using, couldn't keep all the mosquitoes away.

When it comes to fishing, we often have to deal with mosquitoes, flies, or other nasty creatures or elements. Even when we are having fun, there can be some unpleasant aspects.

Life is certainly like that also. Things go wrong, bad things happen to us; we make unwise choices and suffer the consequences. Why does life have to be such a mixture of good and bad?

The Bible tells us why we face nasty pests in life.

"For our struggle is not against flesh and blood, but against the rulers, against the authorities, against the powers of this dark world and against the spiritual forces of evil in the heavenly realms."

Some Christian leaders give the impression that after you become a Christian everything will be nice and smooth in your life. That's not true. We are involved in spiritual warfare. The enemy doesn't like what we are doing and he wants to interfere and make things miserable for us.

We must not despair, though. We are on the winning team! Jesus Christ has won the battle. The enemy has been defeated! And even though we are still in the cleanup phase of the war that has already been won, we don't have to be afraid. If we have invited Jesus, by his Spirit, to come into our lives and be the leader, we can be assured that:

"...the one who is in you is greater than the one who is in the world."

Rely on God's strength when the battle gets tough. ✖◯

REFLECTION

EPHESIANS 6:10-18   1 JOHN 4:4

75

TANGLED LINES

Almost anyone who has used a bait caster has probably had a "rat's nest" or in other words, a really tangled mess! Perhaps the pros never have this problem, but for the rest of us, the boat turns a little and the wind shifts into our face so that the lure doesn't go out so far, and we are left with tangled lines! Or, what's even worse, our lure catches something on the boat as we give one mighty heave. What a grand mess!

If it doesn't seem too bad we may try to untangle the twisted line, but sometimes it's better to take out a knife and start cutting!

Messed up! Confusing!

There were some people in Jesus' day that were dealing with some confusion. Life just didn't make sense for them. The story is told of two men traveling down a road right after Jesus was crucified and then arose from the dead. Jesus joins them as they walk along, although they didn't recognize him right away.

If we review the conversation they had, we can see they were confused.

They were dealing with a "rat's nest" religiously.

"...do you not know the things that have happened here in these days?"

And then they started telling Jesus, not knowing whom they were talking to, what had happened to this person called Jesus. They gave their version of the story, but for them things just didn't make sense. It was so confusing.

Perhaps you are dealing with a situation in your personal or family life that is confusing. Or maybe it is at work. Things might have been going well for a while, but somehow the wind came up just as you were casting, or your lure in life hit a snag, and life for you became confusing and mixed up.

As we further reflect on this passage, one of the most amazing things we see about Jesus is that Jesus meets them in their confusion! And not only does Jesus connect with them in their confusion, he helps them see the bigger picture of the situation.

If your life is mixed up and confusing, remember, Jesus is willing to meet you in your confusion. Not only does he meet you there, he helps you gain a better perspective on what is happening! Will you turn to him in your mess? Meet him there and ask him to help you gain a better perspective on what is happening. ✕◯

REFLECTION

LUKE 24:13-35

BROKEN

How many of us haven't been disappointed with a broken line? The big one got away! We knew when it hit that it was huge! People fly-fishing for salmon or steelhead in the rivers are accustomed to more "break-offs" than landings. When those big bruisers hit and run down stream like a freight train, nothing is going to stop them.

Broken lines, broken equipment, motors don't run, boats have problems, rods break, and reels quit working; we find brokenness is all around. I remember one week of fishing with my extended family. By the end of the week we had only one boat motor working, and that one would only go backwards!

Brokenness comes in many different forms. Many of us have experienced a broken relationship. Some of you are now struggling from the results of a divorce. Others have a strained or broken relationship with a child, a parent, or a friend. Yet others struggle with brokenness due to loss, like in the death of a loved one. With broken relationships we experience a broken heart!

In my own life there have been a variety of times when I have felt broken emotionally, but nothing was as devastating as the loss of our youngest son, at age 16, in an automobile accident. There haven't been any quick fixes and the pain still continues, but I am learning the truth of one statement in the Bible.

God says in the Bible:

"I live in a high and holy place."

No wonder we don't understand all of his ways!

But he doesn't stop there, he goes on to say:

"...but also with him who is contrite and lowly in spirit..."

...which means broken hearted.

Even though grief has been heavy and life is filled with questions that don't have answers, God has become more real than at any other time in my life.

If you feel broken inside and are facing circumstances that are not easily repaired, don't despair! Find a new and deeper relationship with God through this experience. If your life feels empty and worthless, don't give up. Reconnect with the God who has come "down" to live with you! He is close by. Will you connect with him? ✗◯

REFLECTION

ISAIAH 57:15

LOONS

I enjoy watching loons, but what an amazing and mysterious bird. Perhaps those that have studied them intensely understand some of the strange nature of the loon, but most of us are fascinated by this peculiar bird.

Fishing sometimes seems like a mystery. Things are not explainable. They don't seem to make sense. For example, one year we were fishing in Canada. My brothers-in-law invited me to join them with our sons and we headed up to a resort in Ontario.

For months we eagerly anticipated and prepared for this trip. Finally the time came when we could load our

belongings in the car and head north. We drove several hours, and then boarded the train that dropped us off at a certain mile marker. When we stepped out of the train it looked like wilderness area, but upon closer examination, there we some boats at the bottom of the hill waiting for us at the edge of a lake to take us to the resort.

It was beautiful. We couldn't wait to start fishing. We could almost taste some fresh walleye. But we had a problem. We were not catching any walleyes. Once in a while we caught a straggler, but nothing consistently. We tried earlier in the morning and fished until late at night. If you live up there or have been up there, you know there is little night as the sun rises very early and then sets very late in the summer.

I believe it was the third day when we decided to try something else. We took our kids and tried fishing for perch in the middle of the day. We had seen some light grass a short distance from camp, so we thought we would try that first. It wasn't far from camp, so if we got too hot or weren't catching anything we could return to camp for a nap.

We baited the first jig and let it down to the bottom. It didn't take long to get there because we were in an area that was only about 5-7 feet deep. Almost as soon as it hit the bottom, we had a bite. We expected to pull up a nice perch and to our surprise it was a walleye! On that day, we didn't just catch one stray walleye. We limited out on some decent walleyes. It just didn't make sense. I thought walleyes eyes were sensitive and it was a bright sunny day with very little cover in the middle of the summer. Why were we catching walleyes with bright sun in shallow water with little cover in the middle of the day? I still don't understand why this happened or why it kept happening the rest of the week. On every day our best fishing was in the middle of the day in shallow water and all week long the sun was shining.

Life is sometimes mysterious. Why do young people die and old people who want to die still live? Why do some children go to bed without experiencing love while other parents who would love them don't have children? Why do good people have to endure such hardships but other "bad" people seem to enjoy a very smooth and easy life?

I certainly don't have all the answers and when our youngest son was killed in a car accident, it raised more questions than ever before. But somehow in the midst of all this I have concluded that, if God was small enough that we could understand everything about him, he would not be

God. God has a plan that is bigger and more involved than what we can understand, but it is also better in the long run.

> **"The Lord has established his throne in heaven, and his kingdom rules over all."**

If you are facing questions about the mysteriousness of life, don't despair. Bring your questions to God. You may not get answers, but you will still find a God who gives you strength when you are weak, a God who is there when you feel broken, and a God who loves you even when life is not going well.

REFLECTION

PSALM 103:19

QUICKSAND

My son and nephew decided to head out to a local river to do a little trout fishing. It was a nice afternoon and seemed no better way to spend it than fly fishing on the river.

They had a short drive and then arrived at the river. It wasn't the right time of the year to fish for the big steelhead or salmon, but any fly fisherman knows any type of fly fishing is great.

It didn't take long before they landed a few fish. They worked up stream and kept catching trout.

My son moved further up when suddenly he walked into quicksand! Down he went! It wasn't just a hole. He was stuck and was sinking further.

Can you imagine what fear might grip someone at such a moment! Natural emotions - but how quickly they arise!

Thankfully my nephew was close enough and the first thing he could extend to my son was his fishing rod. Even a fly rod can make a difference in a situation like this! My son was able to grab his fly rod and eventually he helped my son to get out.

Fear: It can over take us in an instant! There are many other situations that can cause us to fear. Like when we are out fishing and a violent thunderstorm moves in quickly before we can get off the lake. The lighting seems way to close! Fear comes in dangerous situations, but some of us live with fear every day. We are afraid of what might

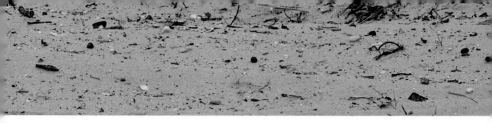

happen in a relationship, or at work, or with our health. We may fear the future in light of what is happening in our world.

In the Bible, God often speaks about fear. God says, "Do not fear." It's not that he is opposed to normal human emotions. He made them. He is talking about fear that lingers; that brings worry.

Listen to what God says in one place in the Bible:

"So do not fear, for I am with you; do not be dismayed, for I am your God. I will strengthen you and help you; I will uphold you with my righteous right hand."

When you are afraid remember what God says. Another verse puts it this way:

"For I am the Lord your God who takes hold of your right hand, and says to you, do not fear; I will help you."

Will you grab on to what God offers when your situation leaves you with concern? ✕〇

REFLECTION

ISAIAH 41:10,13

EXPECTATIONS

We signed up for the fishing tournament and expected to place in the money! We had fished the lake before and recently had been doing very well at catching more than our share of fish. We should have no problem competing at this event. But on the day of the tournament, the fish seemed to have a different idea. We tried the same holes, the same approach and didn't even get one bite! It was not until later in the morning that we sort of "accidentally" picked up two small ones. That hardly seemed enough to bring in to the weigh-in.

How many times haven't you had it when you had huge expectations, but then they were crushed? Perhaps a cold front moved through and fishing never seemed so hard. Or you came to the lake you had fished before and were going to try the same weed beds, only to find no weeds in those areas. The lake association had scheduled treatment or removal of weeds and your favorite beds were gone and you had no idea where the fish had gone.

Expectations. I am learning (and keep learning) that when I expect too much I usually set myself up for a disappointment.

We expect to win the tournament, or at least place in the money. We expect to catch a big fish. We take a family member or friend along, and expect them, on their first time out, to catch a huge fish.

Now I'm not suggesting that we walk around with a dark, gloomy, defeated attitude all day long, but some adjustment of our attitudes might make for more enjoyable living.

In fact, if we have reasonable expectations, we will probably be thankfully surprised when something better happens or something bigger comes our way.

The Bible teaches us to keep things in perspective. We should not say that today or tomorrow we will go here or there or do this amount or type of business or stay for so long...instead we should say:

"If it's the Lord's will, we will live or do this or that."

I have a friend who often reminds me of this. When I ask him how his day is going, he responds something like, "I never have a bad day." He has had a couple of "close calls" and has learned that each day is a gift from God. To be alive is to be thankful.

Perhaps we all need such a reminder, especially if we find ourselves having some disappointing experiences. We may need to adjust our expectations to a more reasonable level. Then we can be thankful when we are surprised beyond our expectations. ✖️◯

REFLECTION

REFLECTION

JAMES 4:13-15

WATCHING AN EAGLE

It was a beautiful June day. We were on a lake in Canada fishing for walleyes. The weather was great and the bugs were not bothering. Besides that, the fish were even biting. As I looked along the tree line bordering the lake, I noticed an eagle flying. What a magnificent bird! The white of its head and tail was so obvious as it floated down and landed in a tree near us. Often in the next few days we watched these majestic birds fly.

As I watched the eagle fly, I particularly noticed two things. First was the power of the wings beating. These massive wings didn't have to beat very much to get the eagle moving through the air. The other thing that I noticed was how at ease the eagle seemed to be as it soared and soared above the trees.

In life we are faced with many challenges and sometimes life just gets tough. Financial security seems to have melted away. We face losses and problems that make us discouraged and depressed. Work has disappeared like a mist in the morning. Some of us have experienced relationships that have gone sour. Life just isn't fun anymore.

The Bible gives a special promise to people in difficult times. The passage begins with words of comfort to a people who in that day were in captivity, having been taken over by a foreign power. God comes and tells them that a change is coming. The Bible then goes on to give a wonderful picture of how great God is and yet how caring he is. It then concludes with these thoughts:

> *"He gives strength to the weary and increases the power of the weak."*

Have you ever run out of emotional energy? Listen to God's promise of what he offers. He is the one who can give us inner strength and help us when we feel weak or exhausted.

The Bible goes on:

"...but those who hope in the Lord will renew their strength. They will soar on wings like eagles; they will run and not grow weary, they will walk and not be faint."

"Those who hope in the Lord," refers to those who keep on trusting in Jesus Christ. We all need to come to a point where we put our trust in Jesus Christ. We need to accept what he has done for us to pay for our sins and invite him to be the leader of our life.

If you haven't done that, you need to start there. This passage goes further when it talks about continuing to trust in him. To keep on trusting in him when the going gets rough. To continue to trust him even when you don't see a change for the better coming.

When we keep on trusting, he promises strength, power like an eagle mounting into the air. When we keep trusting in him, he promises rest, being at ease, like an eagle soaring through the air.

Have you put your trust in him? Will you keep on trusting him? ✖○

REFLECTION

ISAIAH 40:29-31

TILT AND TRIM

Equipment is wonderful when it is working, but it always seems to break down at the wrong time.

We had a weekend planned when we would be using the boat a lot. I took it up to the lake, after it was used in a "Take a Kid Fishing" event put on by a local church. We dropped the boat in the water at the public landing and drove back to the cottage where we would pick up more people.

As we tried to park the boat on shore, we had trouble getting the motor to tip up. Normally we just push the switch on the handle and the motor starts tipping up. This time we had a different response. It made a little noise like it was attempting to do something, and then quit completely. I tried the other two controls (near the front of the boat and also on the motor) with the same result. It was not working!

After getting a screw driver, I was able to manually release the pressure so we could adjust the motor to load it back up on the trailer.

No boating for that weekend. We would have to bring it in for repair. The boat dealer discovered that the tilt and trim motor had run out of steam. It was not working

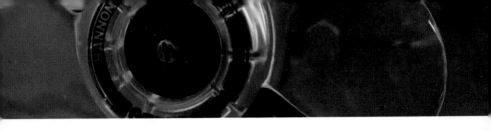

properly. It would have to be rebuilt or replaced.

Sometimes in life we run out of steam. Emotionally we struggle and fail. We get discouraged and even get depressed. Stress builds up and we aren't able to cope well.

In Bible times, I am sure the Psalmist faced times of difficult stress and depressing emotions. He says:

"My flesh and my heart may fail..."

Physically he was exhausted and couldn't go on. But an even deeper paralysis, his emotions failed him. He was worn out, exhausted, broken down inside. His life was unable to work well.

But then he goes on:

"...but God is the strength of my heart."

The author knew that he didn't have the resources within himself to cope, but he found strength to help in tough times. God can help us cope in the toughest times.

How about you? Is life stressful? Are you running out of energy – physically or emotionally? Don't try to muster up more energy. No matter how much we pushed the control, our motor would not tilt. Life is like that. We need help. When you run out of energy, don't just try to get more out of yourself. Turn to God and let Him help you. Depend upon God to give you the strength you need to survive. ✠

REFLECTION

PSALM 73:26

SURPRISE

We had moved from Colorado to Iowa. In Colorado we had gotten used to stream and lake fishing for those beautiful brookies along with some occasional rainbows. Light tackle, small fish, but still what enjoyment!

We moved to Iowa at the beginning of the year in an Iowa blizzard. Not much fishing was going on at that time except for a little ice fishing. In talking to some of the outdoors people who lived in that area, I heard several of them mention a lake nearby that was very good for walleye fishing. They encouraged us to try it the first day of the season.

We waited for that day to come and made some adjustments. We read more about walleye fishing and purchased some lures and equipment that was better suited for that kind of fishing.

Finally opening day came. Before the sun came up, we went out with three of us, my wife, a friend, and me. We were in a 14 foot aluminum boat with a 7 ½ h.p. motor.

We fished one area that was known to be good for walleyes without any success.

After a while our friend suggested that we move to a new area where there was a sunken island. This sounded good to us, so we decided to head that way. Being avid fishermen, we weren't going to waste even one opportunity, so we put on a couple of pike lures and began to troll toward that island.

We had just about reached the island when my wife suddenly hit a snag. Her pole was bent over and it looked like her line was ready to break. I stopped the motor and she tried to wind it in. She pulled and reeled, but nothing happened. It was not moving! We figured we snagged into one of the old logs that had floated into the lake from a previous logging operation.

Eventually my wife got tired fighting this log, so she gave the pole to me. I tightened the drag and started pumping it in. Actually, the snag wasn't moving; instead our boat was moving backwards toward the snag. When we got just about to the place where the line went down I felt it release. I thought the log or branch had given way. It still was a very heavy drag on my line.

When it was about 10 yards from our boat I noticed the log

change. It was heading right toward the boat. Suddenly to my amazement I realized it wasn't a log at all! It was a huge fish! It swam right alongside the boat less than two feet away on the top of the water. The fish extended from the back of the boat to past the middle seat! What a change from fishing for a little brook trout to this monster! Our "snag" was a 40-50 pound muskie!

The fish suddenly decided to head into deeper water. I had to hold on to my pole for all I was worth. Remember, I had tightened the drag as much as I could. Line was just screaming off that reel! Eventually it slowed down and made one more pass coming right by the boat once again! Right next to the boat, probably a foot away on top of the water! What an amazing fish! By that time it must have been annoyed with what was happening, because it took off and my line broke like a tiny little thread!

Surprise – something much bigger and better than what we expect! That's what God says he will do by his spirit working within us!

"Now to him who is able to do immeasurably more than all we ask or imagine, according to his power that is at work within us, to him be glory..."

God says he is able to do more than what we could ever ask for and even more than what we could imagine. Will you trust him to do that in your life? In some area of your life? Talk to him and invite his Spirit to bring pleasant surprises into your life. Don't forget to give him the credit when he answers.
✕◯

REFLECTION
REFLECTION

EPHESIANS 3:20-21

OUTDOORS

We enjoy the out-of-doors. We like to fish, hunt, and/or do a variety of other outdoor activities. It is refreshing to get outside where we can leave our cares behind and be refreshed.

Many of us deal with stressful situations on a daily basis. Our jobs are more and more demanding. The "down economy" affects us more than we realize. We face stressful relationships...

From the Bible, we can we learn something from Jesus Christ about dealing with stress.

Let me share one example. It was an extremely busy day of ministry for Jesus. A large crowd of 5,000 men along with women and children had gathered to hear Jesus teach. The people stayed late into the evening. As it was getting later Jesus told his disciples to feed these people. Then Jesus performed a miracle of feeding them by using only five loaves and two fish. The Bible says that all the people ate until they were satisfied and they still had 12 basketfuls left!

Being in front of a crowd of people and teaching them all day must have been very exhausting for Jesus. Then he fed all 5,000 men, plus women and children. Consider what kind of challenge that must have been. It's hard enough for most of us to keep a family meal going well.

The Bible shows us how Jesus responded to this kind of stress. It tells us that afterwards he got off by himself in the outdoors and prayed. He dismissed the crowd. He told

his disciples to get in the boat and head to a different town. And then the Bible says that Jesus went up on a mountainside to pray.

Jesus often spent time outdoors with God. One passage puts it this way:

> *"But Jesus often withdrew to lonely places and prayed."*

Perhaps you are dealing with a lot of stress. Will you go off to a lonely place?

Will you get away by yourself in nature? Leave your fishing rod or gun at home and don't try to accomplish some other outdoor activity. Instead, go off into the outdoors by yourself, and connect with God. Perhaps it would be difficult for you right now to go to a mountain. But you may be able to take a walk in a park, or just sit in your own backyard, and spend time talking to God about what is going on in your life. Invite him to be a part of what is happening. Connect with him deeply enough until you receive peace about your situation or until you sense a direction you should take.

If Jesus needed to tap into God for strength to go on, how much more don't we need God's help? ✕◯

REFLECTION

REFLECTION

MARK 6:46   LUKE 5:16

FLY-IN FISHING

At a local Sport Fishing Show it is very common to see many booths inviting one to consider a fly-in fishing trip in Canada. Many people from our area have enjoyed the thrill of fishing lakes that can only be reached by plane. These lakes often produce good fishing both in quantities of fish and also in size. Some real trophies are taken from some of these lakes.

One thing each fisherman faces when he plans such a trip is what he can take along. Many people like to avoid getting on a scale, concerned about how much they weigh, but a fly-in fisherman usually has to carefully weigh everything, to make sure he is within the limit allowed.

Weight restrictions often put a limitation on which lures he can bring along. This is especially true if he is pursuing trophy pike. Many of those lures weigh more than other lures, so the pike fisherman must pick and choose which lures to take.

It is sometimes painful leaving behind some favorite lures, because you are restricted by how much weight you can have. Not only does a fly-in fisherman have to leave behind a

few favorite lures, he also must carefully sort through all his baggage to make sure that he has only essential items along. But any fisherman is willing to make those kinds of adjustments to reach the goal he is pursuing.

The Bible shows us the proper goal to pursue for our lives:

> **"Let us fix our eyes on Jesus, the author and perfecter of our faith..."**

Moving on with that goal in mind, also means we need to get rid of some things from our lives. The Bible talks about a process something like this. It says:

> **"Let us throw off everything that hinders and the sin that so easily entangles, and let us run with perseverance the race marked out for us."**

If the fisherman wants to get to that remote lake, he must live by the regulations. The goal he has in mind helps him to leave some things behind.

Think about your life. Where is your life headed? What goal(s) are you focusing on? How much of your life is focused on Jesus Christ? And if that is true or needs to be adjusted, what extra baggage do you need to leave behind? Do you have some unimportant baggage that can be thrown aside? Do you have some improper baggage – sinful thought patterns, language, or lifestyle that you need to get rid of to better pursue the proper goal?

A fisherman eagerly concentrates and thinks about the fly-in fishing trip. We need to remember that we will have a "flight" some day that is far more important than a fishing trip. If we are to make it to heaven, we need to make sure we

have made the right reservation with Jesus, and because of that we are also willing to move in the proper direction with the right baggage. ✗◯

REFLECTION

HEBREWS 12:1-3

WHAT A RUSH

The adrenaline flows. You have just hooked into your biggest fish. Your heart beats faster, your breathing is more rapid, you suddenly warm up or start to sweat; you may even start trembling with excitement. What a thrill! From hooking a huge fish, a record book buck coming out of the swamp into view, or a ruffed grouse explodes from the tree you have just walked under; what a thrilling experience. Outdoor experiences can be amazing!

Some outdoor people get a different kind of rush from something else – from the alcohol they consume. Whether it is stopping after work on the way home, being out with your friends, or attending an event where you have free access, sometimes you find yourself drinking

too much. You put yourself and others at risk if you drive. It is easy to make some bad choices, and the next morning you can't remember what you might have done.

The Bible doesn't forbid drinking (although it may not be wise for a person to drink at all if you are or are with a recovering alcoholic). The Bible tells us not to get drunk.

The Bible says:

"Don't be drunk...Instead, be filled with the Spirit."

If you want to experience another "rush," a good, wonderful, high feeling...don't try to find it in alcohol, but

invite God's Holy Spirit to fill you! You can get a more satisfying rush when God's Spirit enables you to make smart choices, to build up relationships, and to function better in daily living. Doesn't it make more sense to do things God's way? ✜

▌REFLECTION

EPHESIANS 5:18

SWANS

On Michigan's inland lakes it is becoming more and more common to see swans, beautiful, white, lovely birds! But have you ever experienced the temperment of a mute swan?

My son was out fishing with a friend and apparently got their boat too close to the nest of a pair of mute swans. The swans attacked them, swooping down to their boat and they kept pecking at their faces and arms. It was not a pleasant sight; they got out of there as fast as they could with the swans chasing them.

I have some friends who live on a small lake, who enjoy waterfowl hunting. They used to have all kinds of ducks and some geese on their lake. Then a pair of mute swans moved in. They said they watched these swans kill all the baby goslings. One by one the swans would swoop down and pick the little goslings swimming behind their mother and eventually they would kill one. They kept this on for several days until all the babies were gone. They said all the ducks moved out after the swans arrived.

Not all swans are like this, and mutes aren't always mean. But they can get very nasty especially if you get anywhere near their nest.

As I reflected on this, it reminded me of our quest to look good on the outside. Look at how much money is spent to improve our outer appearance. But as the old expression puts it, "looks are only skin deep."

What you are like on the inside is far more important than what you look like on the outside.

I suspect all of us know some very attractive people

who aren't that nice on the inside.

The Bible reminds us that inner beauty is more important. The Bible describes how God sent a prophet to select a new king. God guided him to Jesse's family. Jesse presented his older sons before the prophet. They were mature, certainly it must be one of the oldest. But the prophet knew that God had not chosen one of them to be the next king. He asked if this was all his sons. Jesse said there was one more but he was still young; he was out tending sheep at a more distant place. Jesse didn't think that his youngest son, David, would qualify when the prophet was looking for a king, he was just a kid. The prophet asked for him to be brought. The prophet knew that the Lord had chosen this youngest son. Jesse looked on the outward appearance, but God looked at David's heart. King David was one of the greatest kings that ever lived, and it was from his line that Jesus Christ, the promised Messiah was born!

Where do you focus your energy? Is it all spent on exterior attractiveness? How much energy do you put on developing inner character and inner beauty? ✕◯

REFLECTION

I SAMUEL 16:1-13

SUNGLASSES

Fishermen know that good sunglasses can be very helpful in fishing. For example, in the spring on inland lakes, it is much easier to see where the beds are. When fly fishing, you can read the stream and watch your fly much better with the right sunglasses on. And for those of you who fish tarpon, you know the advantage of seeing the fish before you cast.

When it comes to living, it would be helpful to wear a different pair of glasses.

Too often we get so focused on our own perspective and concerns that we miss seeing what others are going through.

For those of us who have learned to train our eyes to see fish or to read structure, why not train our eyes to see people differently.

Jesus saw people from a different perspective. As Jesus interacted with crowds of people, he noticed something more than what we would see:

> *"When he saw the crowds, he had compassion on them, because they were harassed and helpless, like sheep without a shepherd."*

Jesus could sense the hurt, brokenness, fear and concern of those in the crowd.

Would you be open to a challenge? Ask Jesus to help you see people the way he sees them.

Start with those closest to you, like your spouse, significant other, or a close friend. Ask God to help you see that person the way God sees him or her.

Do the same for other relationships – other family members, friends, fellow workers, fellow board or committee members, or others in your daily circles. I would suggest you even pray something like this the next time you go into a store, "Jesus help me to see at least one person the way you see him/her."

You will be surprised at the new insights you gain as you interact with people if you let God open your eyes. ⊱⊰

REFLECTION

MATTHEW 9:35-38

FISHING LINE

Today we have many choices as to what fishing line we want to use.

Most of us have a preferred brand and weight.

I don't know if you have the same problem as me, but I have found that line seems to tangle a lot quicker these days. No matter how you put it on the reel, it still comes popping off the reel in tangles. I find this especially true in the lighter line when I fish for panfish like crappies.

Certainly companies have made improvements in line. They are stronger, have less weak spots, and are more invisible. It seems though, that some of these improvements have also come with new weaknesses.

Some of us use very light line. If you are fly-fishing, you use a very light weight for the tippet. In inland fishing, we match the weight of the line to the type of fish and cover that we are in. Deep sea fisherman may use heavier line, unless they are fishing a tournament where a specific line weight is important.

Next time you cast out, look at your line. Let the line represent life. Choose one point on the line. The dot that you picked out, is life on this earth. The rest of the line represents eternal life, a life that goes on forever.

When it comes to living on this earth, most of us try to stuff as much as we possibly can into it. We obtain as much as we can. We travel. We enjoy fishing and hunting expeditions. We try not to leave anything out.

It's not wrong to enjoy a full and satisfying life on this earth. After all, Jesus came so that we could have an abundant life, so full that it cannot be contained. It's a life that starts now on this earth and gets even better once we get to heaven.

But we also need to consider storing up treasurers for eternity. How foolish to spend all our time and effort and resources on the dot, instead of on the rest of the line; that is, life on this earth, compared to eternal life that lasts forever.

The Bible says:

> *"Do not store up for yourselves treasurers on earth, where moth and rust destroy, and where thieves break in and steal. But store up for yourselves treasurers in heaven..."*

Seriously consider what kind of investment you are making for life in heaven. ✺

REFLECTION

REFLECTION

JOHN 10:10, 1 TIMOTHY 6:17, MATTHEW 6:19-20

LIGHT MIST

Some of the most beautiful mornings I can remember at the lake are those when I get up early to go fishing and discover a light fog hovering over the water.

The lake is like a mirror as the sun rises.

All around the birds are singing; a robin sings in a nearby tree, a song sparrow adds its tune in the bush by the lake, a red-winged blackbird is adding its pleasant sound from the reeds by the lake, a loon calls out through the mist somewhere in the distance.

One can hear the wing beats of some ducks as they fly low over the water; they bank one more time and land.

A light mist hangs over the lake. It is so light that it appears to be just a vapor sparkling in the sun as it rises. The mist doesn't last long. As the sun rises higher and the temperature increases, the mist disappears.

In many ways life is like that. It seems to fly by so quickly. The Bible talks about life being like a vapor or a mist that

appears for a little while and then vanishes.

The Bible says:

> **"You are a mist that appears for a little while and then vanishes."**

But we do not die and disappear like the mist leaving only memories behind. Life on this earth is just a prelude to eternity.

Are we ready to meet God whenever that time may come?

Have we invested in the future? ✠

REFLECTION
REFLECTION

JAMES 4:14 - MATTHEW 6:19-20

ANTICIPATION

Fishermen live with anticipation. Ice fishermen going after the big pike with a tip-up; eagerly watch to see if the flag is tripped. The same is true whether you are jigging for walleyes or panfish through the ice, or are trying to catch fish in the summer. We eagerly await a bite. We not only hope for a catch, but we anticipate a "big one." Every cast or each time we put down the line, we wait for another hit.

In the Bible we read of people who were anticipating something to happen. They had gotten to know Jesus, heard him teach, saw what he did. They saw him suffer, shed his blood, and die on the cross, and then arise from the dead. A short time after Jesus arose from the dead, he ascended back into heaven. One day as they were standing there, he just went up and disappeared into the clouds. An angel appeared and told them that someday Jesus would come back again. They couldn't wait for that day. They expected it any time. They eagerly anticipated meeting Jesus again!

The Bible shows that Jesus could return at any time. Even if that doesn't happen in our life time, we can be assured that we will all meet God.

How eager are you to meet God?

Most of us get a little uncomfortable or perhaps even scared when we think about meeting God. What will he say? Will he accept us? Why should he let me into his heaven?

If it was based upon how we lived, none of us would stand a chance. In fact, Jesus pointed out that from God's perspective, even thoughts are as bad as the action.

There isn't one of us here who hasn't had some bad thoughts. We have all said some things that we regret. We should have spoken up when we didn't. And we haven't even kept our own moral code perfectly, let alone satisfying a holy, pure, sinless God.

But the good news of the Bible is that we don't have to be afraid of the future, and we can even look forward to the time when we meet God.

When we put our trust in Jesus Christ, accepting what he did as payment for the penalty of our sins, we can experience a new and better life even now. Because he rose from the dead and gives us his spirit to live inside us, he empowers us to live a better life. He will welcome us home when that time comes.

Have you put your trust in him? If not, what is keeping you from doing that? A lot is at stake; why not settle things with him now.

If we have trusted in Christ, let's live in such a way that we are eager to meet him. Let's anticipate that time when he returns or when we go home to be with him forever. ✕◯

Jesus says:

" 'Yes, I am coming soon.'

Amen. Come, Lord Jesus!"

REFLECTION

ACTS 1:1-10   REVELATION 22:20

KID'S FISHING - TIPS

Here are some tips on taking children out fishing, starting at an early age.

x⊃ Make sure it is an enjoyable experience for the child.

x⊃ Include them in the entire process. From planning, shopping for lures, picking up bait, and through the fishing experience.

x⊃ Do what interests them. Most young kids would rather catch several panfish (bluegills, perch, etc.), than spending time going after the "big one." As they get older they may enjoy fishing for bigger game.

x⊃ Realize they have short attention spans. Don't be

concerned if they spend more time catching frogs or butterflies than they do fishing. Fishing will come later.

x⊃ Buy very good equipment that works well and fits them. Nothing can be more discouraging than a reel that doesn't work well, or a pole that is too long or too short.

xo Comfort is very important. Make sure they have warm, bug proofed, water repelent clothes, gloves and boots. Kids tend to get cold much quicker than adults. An experience can turn bad if they are not comfortable.

xo Take along sun screen and bug spray.

xo Point out other aspects of nature.

xo Bring a camera and record memories.

xo Bring water or juice and lots of snacks that they like.

xo Be sensitive to their needs for a bathroom break (choose a place that has facilities).

xo Include a shore lunch if possible. Or stop at one of their favorite restaurants and let them choose what they like.

ABOUT THE AUTHOR

Maury DeYoung is a graduate of Calvin Theological Seminary and has done graduate study at Fuller Theological Seminary. He has been a practicing pastor since 1974. In 1991 Pastor DeYoung, a lifelong outdoorsman, launched an outreach group at his church in Kentwood, Michigan, known as the

 Kelloggsville Church Sportspersons Club. The modest goals of this outreach effort were to help members of the church and their community enjoy fellowship opportunities with others who also enjoy the outdoor lifestyle. Little did Pastor DeYoung realize the grip this outdoor minded club would soon have on his life and the lives of countless others. To say the KCSC grew rapidly is a major understatement. Soon Pastor DeYoung and the Kelloggsville Church had connected with over 9,000 individuals! It wasn't long before Pastor DeYoung found himself mentoring other churches on how they might create similar clubs and reach even more individuals.

In 2004 Sportspersons Ministries International was formed and Pastor DeYoung officially became the driving force behind linking Christians and seekers alike with a wealth of outdoor

fellowship opportunities. The goal of Sportspersons Ministries International is to help individuals of all faith levels build a stronger connection with God. No matter the denomination or the depth of a person's faith, Sportspersons Ministries International uses the common ground of the outdoors as a foundation for building stronger and more meaningful relationships with God. Anyone who has ever marveled at the beauty of nature understands at some level that the natural world in which we live didn't just happen. God created the Earth and all that grows and walks upon it with us in mind. As caretakers, we're all challenged to live the Christian lifestyle that reflects God's will.

Sportspersons Ministries International and Pastor DeYoung challenge individuals of all walks of life to look closer at Christianity. The many hunting, shooting, fishing and other outdoor events they coordinate are the perfect setting for those who love the outdoors to learn more about Christianity and to walk closer with God. They also assist churches in developing similar ministries.

CONTACT INFO

CONTACT INFO

Maury DeYoung is available to speak at your outdoor event, such as a wild game dinner or sportspersons outing.

Maury is also interested in helping you or your church or community start an outdoor ministry.

Please contact Maury at: mdeyoung@spi-int.org
www.spi-int.org